JAY EXPLAINS IT
An In-Depth Presentation
of Claude Hopkins' Classic Book
Scientific Advertising

by

Jay Huling

JAY EXPLAINS IT

An In-Depth Presentation of
Claude Hopkins' Classic Book
Scientific Advertising

JAY HULING

Copyright © 2019 by Jay Huling.

All rights reserved. This book or any portion thereof may not be reproduced or used in any manner whatsoever without the express written permission of the publisher except for the use of brief quotations in a book review or scholarly journal.

First Printing: 2019

ISBN 978-1-79476-698-3

Published by:
The Huling Letter
P.O. Box 14171
Jacksonville, Florida 32238

www.jayhuling.com

Dedication

To everyone who wants their marketing and advertising to get them the exact results they desire.

Forward

You can probably give Claude Hopkins the credit — or the blame — for leading me on the path to becoming the copywriter and consultant I am today.

But the beginning started with my Mother.

There was a "shopper" newspaper called *Bargain Finders* published in my neighborhood and thrown onto everyone's front lawn every other Tuesday morning. It was a compilation of local ads and classifieds — the security alarm companies, water filtration people, HVAC checkups, restaurants, you name it, they were all in there.

One day my Mom saw a help wanted ad in *Bargain Finders*. They were looking for a writer to write "advertorials" for the paper. Advertorials look like articles but are actually paid advertisements. Most newspapers have them, but they are always conspicuously labeled "Paid Advertisement" so the newspaper isn't accused of trying to fool readers.

Bargain Finders had no such concerns.

My Mother sent me over to their offices to apply for the job. I don't recall having a choice or a say-so in the matter. I do remember not wanting to do it, but she always said I would make a good writer... so I went.

It took *Bargain Finders* about five seconds to give me the job — not because I was any good or had any experience. I was the only one who responded to the ad, and they were thrilled that my Mom actually read their paper.

My next step was to try and figure out how to write an advertorial. So my Mom drove me over to a used bookstore called Bookmine, and I looked through the selections hoping to find a "How to Write Advertorials" book. I didn't find anything that specific, but I did get *Scientific Advertising* by Claude Hopkins, *Tested Advertising Methods* by John Caples, *Ogilvy on Advertising* by David Ogilvy, and *Reality in Advertising* by Rosser Reeves. The used, torn up books were cheap, and my Mom is the one who paid for them.

I paid her back, but little did I know at the time I was taking home the Matthew, Mark, Luke, and John of advertising history. As luck would have it, this was the perfect foundation to get started on.

The first one I read was *Scientific Advertising*. I'm not going to be so dramatic and claim it or the other books changed my life. But I was a blank slate that day, and I am thankful for the influence of their wisdom.

And my Mom was very proud. "Did you see Jay's article this week?" she always asked the neighbors. Most of them would politely say yes, even if they hadn't. And some would ask her to ask me to ask *Bargain Finders* to stop throwing their crummy paper in their yard.

I'll be honest — in my humble opinion — as I look back at those first advertorials I wrote... they were good. Not nearly as good as they could've been, but they were really good coming from someone who had never written ads before.

They were good because I learned how to write good ads from Claude Hopkins.

And I remember the satisfaction I received by the feedback I'd get from small business owners who told me the articles were bringing in business and making them money... when other advertising they'd tried had failed to do so.

More than 30 years later, I still feel that satisfaction when my work helps clients make money.

Perhaps not all moms know best. But my Mom did.

Contents

How Advertising Laws Are Established 1

Just Salesmanship 9

Offer Service 17

Mail Order Advertising: What It Teaches 23

Headlines 29

Psychology 35

Being Specific 41

Tell Your Full Story 49

Art in Advertising 55

Things Too Costly 61

Information 67

Strategy 73

Use of Samples 79

Getting Distribution 85

Test Campaigns 91

Leaning on Dealers 97

Individuality 103

Negative Advertising 109

Letter Writing 113

A Name That Helps 119

Good Business 125

CHAPTER

1

How Advertising Laws Are Established

"The time has come when advertising has in some hands reached the status of a science."

And so begins Chapter One of Claude Hopkins' seminal work, *Scientific Advertising*, first published in 1923.

Hopkins was a coveted copywriter back in his day, which is why the advertising agency of Lord & Thomas (now Foote, Cone & Belding) paid him a salary equivalent to $4 million a year in today's dollars.

He was a pioneer of what was then called mail order advertising; what we now call direct response marketing. Hopkins is credited as the first to use sampling, coupons, and money-back guarantees in his propositions. His work for clients such as Schlitz, Pepsodent, Quaker's Puffed Wheat, and Chevrolet is still studied today by advertising scholars and upstarts alike.

Over the years, *Scientific Advertising* has sold 10 million copies. Perhaps the legendary ad man David Ogilvy gave the book its most fitting praise when he claimed:

"Nobody should be allowed to have anything to do with advertising until he has read *Scientific Advertising* seven times. It changed the course of my life."

As I mentioned in my forward, it probably didn't change my life. But I was impressionable enough at that young age to follow Mr. Ogilvy's advice. I read *Scientific Advertising* seven times in a row. And I have reread it several times since. If you apply its principles to today's marketplace, it won't change your business... but it will change how you advertise it.

Hopkins wrote in Chapter One of his book that advertising "is based on fixed principles and is reasonably exact. The causes and effects have been analyzed until they are well understood. The correct methods of procedure have been proved and established. We know what is most effective, and we act on basic laws."

In other words, we know what works... and what doesn't. His statement is still true today.

"Advertising, once a gamble, has thus become, under able direction, one of the safest of business ventures," wrote Hopkins. "Certainly, no other enterprise with comparable possibilities need involve so little risk."

Just like any scientific method, direct response advertising can be observed, examined, and explained in a reproducible way.

Unlike image advertising or branding — the kind that present talking geckos, irrelevant celebrity endorsements, or ads designed solely to create a media buzz — such as

Super Bowl commercials — direct response advertising actually SELLS.

Today's media is quite different from what Hopkins used in his time. But different media doesn't change timeless principles.

Media is just media. Nothing more, nothing less. It is a way to deliver your message to your market. Don't make the mistake of thinking today's media is "different" and therefore requires a different approach. People don't change. They have wants, needs, and desires — regardless of whether the message is presented in a tweet or on a cave wall.

What would Hopkins say about the Internet or Facebook or Twitter or email marketing? The same thing he said about mail order:

"We learn the principles and prove them by repeated tests. This is done through keyed advertising, by traced returns, largely by the use of coupons. We compare one way with many others, backward and forward, and record the results. When one method invariably proves best, that method becomes a fixed principle."

He continues:

"Mail order advertising is traced down to the fraction of a penny. The cost per reply and cost per dollar of sale show up with utter exactness.

"One ad is compared with another, one method with another. Headlines, settings, sizes, arguments and pictures are compared. To reduce the cost of results even one percent means much in some mail order advertising. So no guesswork is permitted. One must know what is best. Thus mail order advertising first established many of our basic laws.

"We offer a sample, a book, a free package or something to induce direct replies. Thus we learn the amount of action which each ad engenders.

"Our final conclusions are always based on cost per customer or cost per dollar of sale."

These words are the bane of the existence of today's so-called "creatives" who strive to win awards, garner likes or re-tweets, or to be lavished with approval from their peers… all at the expense of the client who wants to sell a product or service.

Hopkins' writings from the early 20th century are now a modern-day voice of one crying in the wilderness — "REPENT!"

"No wise advertiser will ever depart from those unvarying laws," wrote Hopkins.

Yet, every day I see these laws broken. The result? TV commercials and radio spots are ignored. Print ads skipped over. Emails deleted. And, yes, direct mail thrown away.

Millions and millions of marketing dollars are wasted year after year.

I often frustrate my clients because I make it clear to them that I don't care what they like, what their spouse likes, what their kids like, or what their employees or peers like.

They only thing I care about is what works for you, gets results for you, and makes money for you.

Just like Claude Hopkins did for his clients.

That's why I've chosen to present my annotated version of *Scientific Advertising* for your benefit and edification.

Let's put these principles to work for you and for your business.

I want you to experience what Hopkins called "the safest, surest ventures which lead to large returns."

CHAPTER

2

Just Salesmanship

> "Advertising is salesmanship," writes Hopkins in Chapter Two. "Its principles are the principles of salesmanship. Successes and failures in both lines are due to like causes."

Remember, this was written back in the early 1920s, before gender-neutral word choice was common. But the idea behind Hopkins' declaration is clear as he continues: "The only purpose of advertising is to make sales. It is profitable or unprofitable according to its actual sales."

Is that your criteria?

Sadly, it's not for a lot of Madison Avenue advertising. Many in the industry — including many small business owners — think advertising is supposed to be "creative." That's their main objective.

Lend me your memory for a second...

Even if you don't remember it, you've probably seen the 1979 Mean Joe Green Coca-Cola TV commercial — because it seems to be on every list of the "World's Greatest TV Commercials." And they show it every year in retrospectives of "Great" Super Bowl ads.

The injured football player limps into the stadium tunnel, headed toward the locker room. He's snarling at having to leave the game, in pain and frustration.

And — what do you know — standing there is a kid with a Coke.

The kid offers Mean Joe a drink, who takes a big swig, and then gives the kid his game-worn football jersey, as a way of saying thanks.

"Greatest TV spot — ever!" the critics claimed. People talked about it, comedy shows parodied it, wannabe ad writers were inspired by it.

And Coke pulled the ad.

Why?

Simple, the ad wasn't selling Coke. Sales actually went down because of it.

Why? It doesn't matter why — although Claude Hopkins could have predicted it way back in 1923. What matters are the sales numbers, which don't lie and don't spin and don't make excuses. Sales were down for Coke, period.

But to this day, the Mean Joe Green Coke spot is revered by people in the advertising industry as one of the all-time greats.

Because they don't know — or don't believe — what YOU need to understand:

Marketing is supposed to make you money.

It's an investment. You invest a dollar, and it better make you a dollar... better yet, 10 dollars, 100 dollars, as much as you can make it make you.

Let's let Hopkins continue:

"Treat it as a salesman. Force it to justify itself. Compare it with other salesmen. Figure its cost and result. Accept no excuses."

He has a lot to say in Chapter Two on the matter. So, I'll give you the highlights here:

- "There is one simple and right way to answer many advertising questions. Ask yourself, 'Would this help a salesman sell the goods?' Would it help me sell them if I met the buyer in person?'"

- "When one tries to show off, or does things merely to please himself, he is little likely to strike a chord which leads people to spend money."

- "Some argue for slogans, some like clever conceits. Would you use them in personal salesmanship? Can you imagine a customer whom such things would impress? If not, don't rely on them for selling in print."

- "Some say, 'Be very brief. People will read but little.' Would you say that to a salesman? With a prospect standing before him, would you confine him to any certain number of words? That would be an unthinkable handicap."

- "Measure them by salesmen's standards, not by amusement standards. Ads are not written to entertain. When they do, those entertainment seekers are little likely to be the people whom you want."

All of these points from Hopkins diagnose what was wrong with the clever Coke ad.

If the producers of that TV spot had bothered to read *Scientific Advertising,* they would have seen the error of their ways before they stepped in it… and wasted so much money.

All of the advertising agencies, freelancers — and even your employees — that you have hired could have saved you a lot of wasted advertising dollars if they had understood these principles.

And they could have made you so much more money by using scientifically proven advertising methods.

But they didn't want to, They wanted to be creative. They wanted to impress people. They wanted to use your money to further their own careers.

Or they simply didn't know any better.

Either way, YOU are the one who gets punished for their malpractice.

And, quite frankly, you have to blame yourself for hiring them. But it doesn't have to be that way from now on.

Hopkins instructions are clear:

"When you plan and prepare an advertisement, keep before you a typical buyer... in everything be guided by what you would do if you met the buyer face-to-face. If you are a normal man and a good salesman, you will then do your level best."

He wasn't just singling out print ads. He was talking about all marketing media. Today, you can apply it to TV, radio, email marketing, Facebook, etc.

And, of course, direct mail.

A lot of people make the mistake of thinking I only push direct mail. That's not true. I only care about the specific media that works for your specific needs of matching your messages to your market.

Your success depends on doing that to the exclusion of everything else.

CHAPTER

3

Offer Service

"Remember that the people you address are selfish," wrote Hopkins in Chapter Three. "They care nothing about your interest or your profit. They seek service for themselves. Ignoring this fact is a common mistake and a costly mistake in advertising."

Yes, direct marketing is supposed to sell stuff. But if your sales proposition can be described as "Give me your money" advertising, you're not going to appeal to many people.

Hopkins knew better.

"Good ads are based entirely on service. They offer wanted information. They cite advantages to users. Perhaps they offer a sample, or to buy the first package, or to send something on approval, so the customer may prove the claims without any cost or risk. Some of these ads seem altruistic. But they are based on a knowledge of human nature. The writers know how people are led to buy."

I often talk about direct mail "attracting" prospects... pulling them in rather than pushing them away... like bees to honey.

Or as Hopkins would describe it, like "salesmanship."

"The good salesman does not merely cry a name. He doesn't say buy my article. He pictures the customer's side of his service until the natural result is to buy."

Most ads you see today are not "good salespeople."

Selling is the unique power of direct mail. You can make a complete sales pitch. You can tell all of your story — in one page or in 64 pages or more — however many pages you need.

Which begs the question I am always asked:

"Is anyone really going to read ALL of that?"

And my answer is to ask you the following question: Is your goal to get people to read or to get people to buy?

If your answer is "to get people to buy," you should give your prospect all of the information they want and need to make a buying decision.

Of course, there is a big difference in buying, say, an engagement ring versus buying a box of paper clips. So you need to use the selling argument appropriate to your situation.

- How much emotion is involved in the purchase?
- How much time, effort, and thought goes into the purchase?

- How expensive is the product or service you're selling?

- How much of a value proposition do you need to present?

- How many objections do you need to overcome?

- How familiar is your prospect with you and with what you're selling?

- How much does your prospect need what you're selling versus how much do they want it?

If they just want it — but don't really need it — you are going to have to use more copy to sell it.

Paper clips or thumb tacks might sell themselves. However, things such as life insurance policies, vacation packages, luxury automobiles, IT systems, collectibles, high-end jewelry, real estate, career training, fundraising — and way too many others to list here — all require long copy because of the degree of involvement required.

And the involvement must appeal to the prospect's self-interest.

Forget about your wants, needs, and desires for a moment and consider those of the prospect's — as Claude Hopkins advised:

"People can be coaxed but not driven. Whatever they do they do to please themselves. Many fewer mistakes would be made in advertising if these facts were never forgotten."

I want to help ensure you don't make those mistakes.

And one of the first things I'm going to do is have an honest conversation with you about your business and your market.

And I'm going to make sure you understand that no one cares about you.

They don't care about your product or service. They don't care about your business. They don't care about your "mission."

They care about themselves.

"What do I get? How do I get it? What will it do for me?"

If your answers to those questions are better and more appealing than your competitor's answers, you'll win.

And winning is what *Scientific Advertising* is all about.

CHAPTER

4

Mail Order Advertising: What It Teaches

Today, we call it direct response marketing.

Back in Claude Hopkins' day, it was referred to as mail order advertising. And it was a lot harder.

Think about it — Claude needed someone to cut the coupon out of an ad or fill out the reply card in a direct mail package. Then, that prospect needed to write a check or get a money order, fill out an envelope, take it all to the post office, put a stamp on it, mail it, and wait six weeks to get whatever was being ordered.

Not today. Today you can drive people to a website. You can call a toll-free number and order. There is FedEx shipping, and you can get your order the next day.

But the principles he talks about in this chapter still hold true.

One of the brute strengths of direct response marketing is its accountability. You either get results or you don't.

You can't be bamboozled by some "creative" executive from an advertising agency schmoozing you about "new matrix" or Facebook likes or "traffic" or website hits or "brand development."

No, direct marketing is all about wins and losses.

Let's let Claude Hopkins explain it:

"The severest test of an advertising man is in selling goods by mail. But that is a school from which he must graduate before he can hope for success. There cost and result are immediately apparent. False theories melt away like snowflakes in the sun. The advertising is profitable or it is not, clearly on the face of returns. Figures which do not lie tell one at once the merits of an ad… All guesswork is eliminated."

Hopkins had other choice words to say about mail order advertising, such as:

- "Every wasted dollar adds to the costs of results."
- It's a "master who can't be fooled."
- "It is the best advertising yet discovered."

"Mail order advertising," Hopkins preached, "tells a complete story if the purpose is to make an immediate sale. You see no limitations there on amount of copy. The motto is:

The more you tell, the more you sell.

"And it has never failed to prove out so in any test we know.

"Sometimes the advertiser uses small ads, sometimes large ads. None are too small to tell a reasonable story. But an ad twice larger brings twice the returns. A four-times-larger ad brings four times the returns, and usually some in addition."

If you talk to the image advertisers — the purveyors of brand and branding — they will likely tell you that copy is ugly.

Here is Hopkins' wise response:

"You may say they are unattractive, crowded, hard to read — anything you will. But the test of results has proved those ads the best salesmen those lines have yet discovered. And they certainly pay... Mail order ads are models. They are selling goods profitably in a difficult way. It is far harder to get mail orders than to send buyers to the stores. It is hard to sell goods which can't be seen. Ads which do that are excellent examples of what advertising should be... Every departure from those principles adds to our selling cost. Therefore, it is always a question of what we are willing to pay for our frivolities."

How much are you willing to pay for your frivolities?

When you sacrifice sales copy for brand images, how much is that costing you? When you limit your letter to one page instead of the four pages you really need to tell your story, how much is that costing you?

If you really think a picture is worth a thousand words, how much is that costing you?

Claude Hopkins understood the client's human nature of wanting things to "look good." He expressed it this way:

"Most of us can afford to do something for pride and opinion. But let us know what we are doing. Let us know the cost of our pride. Then, if our advertising fails to bring the wanted returns, let us go back to our model — a good mail order ad — and eliminate some of our waste."

If you and I work together, I'm not going to be particularly concerned if your advertising looks good.

If we need it to look good to help it sell, that's what we are going to do. But we are not going to take away the selling power to please anyone's aesthetic sensibilities.

If that's what you want, you and I will never agree.

I'm going to help you cut the fat and cut the waste out of your marketing budget. I'll develop a direct marketing program for you that will get you the results you want.

That's what I'm all about.

CHAPTER

5

Headlines

"The salesman is there to demand attention. He cannot well be ignored. The advertisement can be ignored."

"**The difference between advertising and personal salesmanship lies largely in personal contact,**" writes Claude Hopkins in Chapter Five of *Scientific Advertising*.

However, as Hopkins astutely observes, the salesperson wastes a lot time on prospects who have no interest in buying.

Not so with direct mail.

Because direct mail is **TARGETED** direct response marketing.

You can obtain a list of prospects who meet the exact criteria of people who want to buy what you are selling.

You can pick them out of the crowd, so to speak. Hopkins teaches the fundamentals of getting attention — which all starts with a good headline.

In direct mail, the headline on an envelope is often called a teaser. In radio, it's the first sentence you hear. On TV, it's the opening visual that grabs you.

Regardless of the media, an effective headline will:

- Get attention
- Target the audience
- Deliver a complete message
- And draw the prospect into the rest of the ad

Most products and services can't be sold effectively in a single sentence or headline. In such cases, getting the reader to understand and respond to your sales pitch requires the reader to read or at least skim the body copy. You should use your headline as a lure that hooks readers and draws them into the body copy.

And, remember, you only care about the views and interests of buyers. Non-buyers shouldn't be considered, as Hopkins explains:

"What you have will interest certain people only, and for certain reasons. You care only for those people. Then create a headline which will hail those people only."

He also warns against clever headlines:

"Perhaps a blind headline or some clever conceit will attract many times as many. But they may consist mostly of impossible subjects for what you have to offer. And the people you are after may never realize that the ad refers to something they may want."

Here are more words of wisdom from Hopkins in Chapter Five:

People pick out what they wish to read by headlines, and they don't want those headlines to be misleading.

People do not read ads for amusement. They don't read ads which, at a glance, seem to offer nothing interesting.

People are hurried. The average person worth cultivating has too much to read. They skip three-fourths of the reading matter which they pay to get. They are not going to read your business talk unless you make it worth their while and let the headline show it.

People will not be bored in print. They may listen politely at a dinner table to boasts and personalities. But in print they choose their own companions, their own subjects. There may be products which interest them more than anything else. But they will never know it unless the headline or the picture tells them.

"The best of salesmanship has no chance whatever unless we get a hearing," Hopkins preaches. "It is not uncommon for a change in headlines to multiply returns from five to ten times over. So we compare headlines until we know what sort of appeal pays best."

That's why I teach my clients to test. We can send out two different versions of a mailing and see by each one's results which is the better appeal.

Let the market tell you what they want and how to sell it to them.

Claude Hopkins knew that anyone who tests and measures their response will be amazed at the different results they achieve.

"The appeals we like best will rarely prove best, because we do not know enough people to average up their desires," said Hopkins. "Address the people you seek, and them only."

This advice applies to whatever media you use to deliver your message. And it will apply to whatever media is invented in the future that doesn't exist today.

If it ever becomes possible to send your thoughts directly into the mind of your prospect's thoughts via extra sensory perception, you'll still need to get their attention, communicate your message, and call them to action.

Give people what they want, and you'll get what you want.

CHAPTER

6

Psychology

Direct response marketing is all about the art of persuasion. So, the more you know about psychology, the better.

Claude Hopkins writes about the psychology of advertising in Chapter Six. He delves into simple cause and effect, and how you can use that knowledge to increase results and avoid mistakes.

Let's let him explain it:

"Curiosity is one of the strongest of human incentives. We employ it whenever we can... Cheapness is not a strong appeal. Americans are extravagant. They want bargains but not cheapness. They want to feel that they can afford to eat and have and wear the best. Treat them as though they could not and they resent your attitude."

Hopkins notes several stories of success with psychology in Chapter Six. Some of those stories include:

- How visitors to the British National Gallery often pass by a certain painting... until they later are told it is worth $750,000. Then, they go back to look at it.

- A department store whose most popular and bestselling item was a $1,000 Easter bonnet. And, remember, this was back in the 1920s.

- The advertiser who encouraged his prospects to try other brands by his competition. He found buyers wanted the brand so superior that it wasn't afraid of competition.

- The tale of two competitors selling the same item. One tried to give his promotional item away for free. And couldn't. The other "bought the item" for his customers — and promptly sold out of what he was selling. As Hopkins put it, "It is vastly different to pay 15 cents to let you try an article than to simply say it's free."

Hopkins knew that handing an unwanted product to someone will gain you little. They are in no mood to see your virtues. But if you can get your prospect to ask for a sample after reading your story, then they can accept you.

Let's let Claude explain more:

"There is a great deal in mental impression. Submit five articles exactly alike and five people may each choose one of them. But point out in one some qualities to notice and everyone will find them. The five people then will all choose the same article. If people can be made sick or well by mental impressions, they can be made to favor a certain brand in that way. And that, on some lines, is the only way to win them."

And if you get nothing else from this chapter, get this:

"When someone knows that something belongs to them — something with their name on it — they will make the effort to get it, even though the thing is a trifle... Those who are entitled to any seeming advantage will go a long way not to lose that advantage."

Today, we call this **lead generation marketing**. It's all about getting the prospect to "raise their hand" and show you they are interested in what you sell.

Then you can better focus your marketing dollars targeting only people who have told you they want to buy from you.

That's how you find prospects... seemingly out of thin air.

I can help you craft irresistible selling propositions to communicate... so people are compelled to buy from you.

And I can help you put it all together in an affordable way that meets your needs, meets your budget, and gets you the results you want.

CHAPTER

7

Being Specific

None but those who regard advertising as some magic dreamland will ever try to sell without specifics.

In Chapter Seven, Hopkins offers one of his most famous and most quoted sayings of his career:

"Platitudes and generalities roll off the human understanding like water from a duck. They leave no impression whatever. To say, Best in the World, Lowest Prices in Existence, etc., are at best simply claiming the expected. But superlatives of that sort are usually damaging. They suggest looseness of expression, a tendency to exaggerate, a carelessness of truth. They lead readers to discount all the statements that you make."

Yes, prospects know that salespeople put their best foot forward. We're all savvy to the use of exaggeration in advertising. The advertisers certainly like it — and so do their agencies — but the customer is rarely fooled.

Hopkins continues:

"General statements count for little. And a man inclined to superlatives must expect that his every statement will be taken with some caution. But a man who makes a specific claim is either telling the truth or a lie... Actual figures are not generally discounted. Specific facts, when stated, have their full weight and effect... The weight of an argument may often be multiplied by making it specific."

And then Hopkins gives these examples:

A dealer may say, "Our prices have been reduced" without creating any marked impression. But when he says, "Our prices have been reduced 25 percent" he gets the full value of his announcement.

A mail order advertiser sold women's clothing. For years he used the slogan, "Lowest prices in America." His rivals all copied that. Then he guaranteed to undersell any other dealer. His rivals did likewise. Soon those claims became common to every advertiser in his line, and they became commonplace. Then, under able advice, he changed his statement to "Our net profit is 3 percent." That was a definite statement and it proved very impressive. With their volume of business it was evident that their prices must be minimum. No one could be expected to do business on less than 3 percent. The next year their business made a sensational increase.

At one time in the automobile business there was a general impression that profits were excessive. One well-advised advertiser came out with the statement, "Our profit is 9 percent." Then he cited actual costs on the hidden parts of a $1,500 car. They amounted to $735, without including anything one could easily see. This advertiser made a great success along those lines at that time.

I remind you, again, Hopkins was writing in the 1920s. Think about what these numbers mean in today's prices.

Yet, here is another story he tells in *Scientific Advertising* that could teach a lot of Super Bowl advertisers a thing or two.

Imagine if they'd heed his admonishing in this recount:

"In the old days all beers were advertised as **Pure**. The claim made no impression. The bigger the type used, the bigger the folly. After millions had been spent to impress a platitude, one brewer pictured a plate glass room where beer was cooled in filtered air. He pictured a filter of white wood pulp through which every drop was cleared. He told how bottles were washed four times by machinery. How he went down 4,000 feet for pure water. How 1,018 experiments had been made to attain a yeast to give beer that matchless flavor. And how all the yeast was forever made from that adopted mother cell. All the claims were such as any brewer might have made. They were mere essentials in ordinary brewing. But he was the first to tell the people about them, while others cried merely pure beer. He made the greatest success that was ever made in beer advertising."

One statement may take as much room as another, yet a definite statement may be many times as effective. The difference is vast. If a claim is worth making, make it in the most impressive way.

Specific claims when made in print are taken at their value.

Today, marketing people call this the Unique Selling Proposition (USP). Hopkins never called it that. The USP was coined by Rosser Reeves in his book *Reality in Advertising* in 1961.

However, Hopkins would have agreed with what Reeves said:

- Each advertisement must make a proposition to the consumer.

- The proposition must be one that the competition either cannot, or does not, offer.

- The proposition must be so strong that it can move the mass millions, i.e., pull over new customers to your product.

- This is not a uniqueness of the product, but it assumes uniqueness, and cloaks itself in uniqueness, as a claim.

So forget about trying to be unique. Chances are, the truth is you are not unique. And the marketplace knows it. What your proposition needs to say is, "If you get my product, you will get this specific benefit."

In other words, it's a promise.

The promise must be strong. It must be a difference that is very important to the reader.

Why, as Hopkins observes numerous times in *Scientific Advertising,* do so many marketers fail? One reason is that the marketer has not formulated a selling proposition that is irresistible to the prospect. They simply look and sound like everyone else.

The prospect wants to know, "Why should I buy what you have to sell? What am I going to get?"

Your answer must be an advantage the customer really cares about.

You must get your irresistible proposition into the minds of the people most likely to buy the product. And you want to do that in a way that is most affordable to you.

Once you have a marketing machine in place that is reaching the right people with the right message through the right media at a profitable price for you, then you can afford to outspend your competition.

It's like finding a slot machine in Las Vegas that pays you $10 for every $1 you put into it. As long as you are making money, you want to keep feeding that machine.

Your competition won't be able to keep up.

I can help you create that machine.

CHAPTER

8

Tell Your Full Story

Chapter Eight of Scientific Advertising is so important — so relevant to today's direct response marketing world — that it's almost sacrilegious to edit it.

Here's the best of the best:

Whatever claim you use to gain attention, you should tell a reasonably complete story. If you measure your results, you will find that certain claims appeal far more than others. But in usual lines a number of claims appeal to a large percentage. Then present those claims in every ad for their effect on that percentage.

Some marketers, for the sake of brevity, present one claim at a time. Or they write a serial ad, continued in another issue. There is no greater folly. Those serials almost never connect.

When you once get a person's attention, then is the time to accomplish all you ever hope with him. Bring all your good arguments to bear. Cover every phase of your subject. One fact appeals to some, one to another. Omit any one and a certain percentage will lose the fact which might convince.

Present to the prospect every important claim you have.

The best marketers do that. They learn their appealing claims by tests — by comparing results from various headlines. Gradually they accumulate a list of claims important enough to use. All those claims appear in every ad thereafter.

The advertisements seem monotonous to the men who read them all. A complete story is always the same. But one must consider that the average reader is only once a reader, probably. And what you fail to tell him in that ad is something he may never know.

Some advertisers go so far as to never change their ads. Single mail order ads often run year after year without diminishing returns. So with some general ads. They are perfected ads, embodying in the best way known all that one has to say. Advertisers do not expect a second reading. Their constant returns come from getting new readers.

Any reader of your marketing is interested, else they would not be a reader. You are dealing with someone willing to listen. Then do your level best. That reader, if you lose him now, may never again be a reader.

You are like a salesman in a busy man's office. He may have tried again and again to get entree. He may never be admitted again. This is his one chance to get action, and he must employ it to the fullest.

This again brings up the question of brevity. The most common expression you hear about advertising is that people will not read much. Yet a vast amount of the best-paying advertising shows that people do read much. Then they write for a book, perhaps — for added information.

There is no fixed rule on this subject of brevity. One sentence may tell a complete story on a line like chewing gum. It may not on an article like Cream of Wheat. But, whether long or short, an advertising story should be reasonably complete.

Never be guided in any way by ads which are untraced. Never do anything because some uninformed advertiser considers that something right.

Apply to your advertising ordinary common sense. Take the opinion of nobody, the verdict of nobody, who knows nothing about his returns.

As I told you earlier, I don't believe in opinions. I believe in what the marketplace tells us by their votes — and they vote with their response.

You don't have to guess about what will work in your marketing.

I can build you a direct response marketing machine that will prove itself... and get you results every time.

CHAPTER

9

Art in Advertising

Claude Hopkins begins this chapter by saying, "Pictures in advertising are very expensive."

Now, **today, there are cheaper alternatives — stock photography, taking your own digital photos, etc.**

But what Hopkins was really talking about is the "alternative cost" of the space photos and illustration take in a promotion.

Here's what he has to say:

"Pictures should not be used merely because they are interesting. Or to attract attention. Or to decorate an ad. We have covered these points elsewhere. Ads are not written to interest, please or amuse. You are not writing to please the hoi-polloi. You are writing on a serious subject — the subject of money-spending.

"Use pictures only to attract those who may profit you. Use them only when they form a better selling argument than the same amount of space set in type."

And elsewhere he continues:

"Advertising pictures should not be eccentric. Don't treat your subject lightly. Don't lessen respect for yourself or your article by any attempt at frivolity. People do not patronize a clown... An eccentric picture may do you serious damage. One may gain attention by wearing a

fool's cap. But he would ruin his selling prospects…
A picture which is eccentric or unique takes attention from your subject. You cannot afford to do that. Your main appeal lies in your headline. Over-shadow that and you kill it. Don't, to gain general and useless attention, sacrifice the attention that you want."

Hopkins always — and smartly — goes back to the analogy of the salesperson.

"Don't be like a salesman who wears conspicuous clothes. The small percentage he appeals to are not usually good buyers. The great majority of the sane and thrifty heartily despise him. Be normal in everything you do when you are seeking confidence and conviction… The picture must help sell the goods. It should help more than anything else could do in like space, else use that something else."

Regardless of the times Hopkins was writing in, his words ring true today. His "rules" still apply. Do nothing to merely interest, amuse, or attract. "That is not your province," he would say. "Do only that which wins the people you are after in the cheapest possible way."

When selecting visuals, keep these guidelines in mind:

- Don't force visuals.
- The simplest visuals are often the best.
- It's OK not to have a visual at all. Often all-text gives you the most selling power.

- It's OK to use existing photography or stock photos when you can, because this saves you money — and original photos do not necessarily boost your response.

I know Claude Hopkins would be pleased with the work I do for my clients, as he ends this chapter by saying:

"Some things you do may cut all your results in two. Other things can be done which multiply those results. Minor costs are insignificant when compared with basic principles… The great question is, one's power to get the maximum results."

Maximum results — that's what I aim to help you achieve.

You can decide if you want to leave money on the table; if you don't want to get the most bang for your buck.

But if you leave it up to me, I'm going to get you every dollar I can get you.

CHAPTER

10

Things Too Costly

"Many things are possible in advertising which are too costly to attempt. That is another reason why every project and method should be weighed and determined by a known scale of cost and result."

Such **practical wisdom from Claude Hopkins; yet, how many follow his advice?**

Changing people's habits is very expensive. But countless advertisers try to do just that — and much of the advertising is wasted because it goes to people who have already been converted.

In Chapter Ten, Hopkins gives several examples:

"An advertiser at one time spent much money to educate people to the use of oatmeal. The results were too small to discover. All people know of oatmeal. As a food for children it has age-old fame. Doctors have advised it for many generations. People who don't serve oatmeal are therefore difficult to start. Perhaps their objections are insurmountable. Anyway, the cost proved to be beyond all possible return."

"No one orange grower or raisin grower could attempt to increase the consumption of those fruits. The cost might be a thousand times his share of the returns. But thousands of growers combined have done it on those and many other lines. There lies one of the great possibilities of advertising development. The general consumption of scores of foods can be profitably increased. But it must be done through wide cooperation."

"Costly mistakes are made by blindly following some ill-conceived idea. An article, for instance, may have many uses, one of which is to prevent disease. Prevention is not a popular subject, however much it should be. People will do much to cure a trouble, but people in general will do little to prevent it. This has been proved by many disappointments."

Hopkins refers to this approach as "covering a hundred useless readers to reach the one you want."

His entire point is this:

A Buyer is a Buyer is a Buyer.

What I mean by that is, I target prospects for you who have already shown by their buying behavior that they are interested in what you sell.

I can help you find lists for buyers who fit the profile you want.

I can help you change your messages within your marketing to appeal to the exact wants, needs, and desires of each individual prospect.

I can help you stop wasting money on prospects who are not really prospects at all.

Direct response marketing isn't something you should guess at. You should use all the best information you can to make an informed decision.

I can help you get that information.

This chapter, like every chapter, points out a very important reason for knowing your results. Scientific advertising is impossible without that. So is safe advertising. So is maximum profit.

As Claude Hopkins would tell us:

"Groping in the dark in this field has probably cost enough money to pay the national debt. That is what has filled the advertising graveyards. That is what has discouraged thousands who could profit in this field."

You know what to do, but are you willing to do it? Are you willing to have scientific advertising that makes you money?

CHAPTER

11

Information

"An ad writer, to have a chance at success, must gain full information on his subject."

Right off the bat, in Chapter Eleven, Hopkins presents the one thing YOU can do to make my work more successful for you...

...Give me as much information as you can.

Because that's where the ideas come from. That's where the "hidden gold" is buried. I can find that fascinating selling point, that irresistible proposition, the thing which will make the prospect say yes... that others have overlooked.

"Genius is the art of taking pains," was Hopkins' poetic way of stating it. "The advertising man who spares the midnight oil will never get very far."

He continues:

"Every advertiser of a similar product is researched for his literature and claims. Thus we start with exact information on all that our rivals are doing."

And then he makes arguably the most important point in the chapter; so, don't dare miss it:

"It is often necessary in a line to learn the total expenditure. We must learn what a user spends a year, else we shall not know if users are worth the cost of getting... We must learn the total consumption; else we may overspend... We must learn the percentage of readers to whom our product appeals. We must often gather this data on classes. The percentage may differ on farms and in cities. The cost of advertising largely depends on the percentage of waste circulation."

Today, we call this **target marketing**.

I want to help you target the exact prospects who are ready, willing, and able to buy your product or service.

Non-prospects are of no concern to you. Because we want to eliminate as much marketing waste — and waste of your budget — as possible.

I ask a lot of questions, hunting, searching, digging for the right ways to persuade your audience to buy from you.

- What are all the product benefits?

- What are all the features of the product?

- How is the product different and, hopefully, better than the competition?

- What does the buyer expect?

- What methods, approaches and sales techniques are the competition using?

- How is the audience different?

- How much does the buyer expect to pay? And why is the product cheaper or more expensive?

- Can you expect to get multiple sales from the buyer?

- What is the logical "back end" product to sell someone after the purchase?

- What should the tone of my copy be?

- Should we test copy approaches?

- Are testimonials available from satisfied customers?

- Which appeals have worked in the past for this product?

- What objections might arise from a prospective customer? How can we overcome these objections?

- Can we tie in the copy to some news event?

- Can we tie the copy to some holiday or seasonal event?

- Should we use a one-step sales approach or a multi-step approach?

- What can we do to give the reader a sense of urgency so he or she will buy the product now?

- What unsuccessful approaches have been used to sell this product?

- Are we targeting the right amount of people — not too many — so you aren't overwhelmed by the response?

And many more questions — too numerous to list here.

Claude Hopkins summed it up this way:

"Thus an advertising campaign is usually preceded by a very large volume of data. Even an experimental campaign, for effective experiments cost a great deal of work and time."

Persuasive copy gives readers useful information about the product or service. The more facts you include, the better. Writers who don't have facts often fall back on fancy phrases and puffed-up expressions to fill the empty space on the page. The words are pretty, but that's about it.

Give me all previously published material on your product or service. I can most likely glean everything I need from these pieces. The rest I'll get from asking you questions. Digging for the facts always pays off because specifics sell.

Give me your information, and I'll get you the customers you want.

CHAPTER

12

Strategy

"Advertising is like a game of chess," Hopkins tells us in the Chapter Twelve. "We are usually out to capture others' citadels or garner others' trade."

It's a basic understanding of the marketplace. Someone right now already has your customer.

Your prospect can keep buying from your competitor.

They could switch to you.

Or they could keep doing nothing.

That's right. You are also in competition with the prospect doing nothing.

"We must have skill and knowledge," explains Hopkins. "We must have training and experience, also right equipment. We must have proper ammunition, and enough. We dare not underestimate opponents… We also need strategy of the ablest sort, to multiply the value of our forces."

Hopkins covers a lot of ground in Chapter Twelve. Some of his most important points include:

"Often the right name [of a product] is an advertisement in itself. It may tell a fairly complete story. Many a name has proved to be the greatest factor in an articles success."

Back in his day, Hopkins was referring to products such as Shredded Wheat, Cream of Wheat, Puffed Rice, Spearmint Gum, Palmolive Soap, and Corn Flakes.

"Many coined names without meaning have succeeded. Kodak, Karo, Mazda, etc., are examples. They are exclusive. The advertiser who gives them meaning never needs to share his advantage."

"A significant name which helps to impress a dominant claim is certainly a great advantage. Names which tell stories have been worth millions of dollars. So a great deal of research often precedes the selection of a name."

"A product which costs more than the ordinary is considered above the ordinary. So the price question is always a very big factor in strategy."

"Competition must be considered. What are the forces against you? What have they in price or quality or claims to weigh against your appeal? What have you to win trade against them? What have you to hold trade against them when you get it?"

Such things are not accomplished by haphazard efforts. You must consider individuals, typical people who are using rival brands.

This is something general advertising and image advertising can't do effectively. Only direct response marketing can target your most likely prospect, use variable data to customize the exact message they need to receive, and measure your response so you can always adjust your strategies to win.

There is nearly always something impressive which others have not told. Our job in direct response marketing is to discover it. You must present an advantage to your prospect.

As Hopkins put it, "People don't quit a habit without reason." Right now, your prospect has the habit of buying from someone else — or buying from no one — not you.

"These are samples of the problems which advertising men must solve," writes Hopkins. "These are some of the reasons why vast experience is necessary. One oversight may cost the client millions in the end. One wrong piece of strategy may prohibit success. Things done in one way may be twice as easy, half as costly, as when done another way.

"Advertising without this preparation is like a waterfall going to waste. The power may be there, but it is not made effective. We must center the force and direct it in a practical direction.

"Advertising often looks very simple. Thousands of men claim ability to do it. And there still is a wide impression that many men can. As a result, much advertising goes by favor. But the men who know realize that the problems are as many and as important as the problems in building a skyscraper. And many of them lie in the foundations."

Do you think the marketplace is fair?

The marketplace is vast and complicated. The reasons people make buying decisions are not cut and dry. Copywriters who get results for their clients know all the nuances, history, precedents, persuasion tactics, and tricks to deliver an outcome their client wants.

When you hire someone and their stuff doesn't work for you, that's expensive. When you hire me and I make you money, it doesn't really cost you anything at all.

Paying for the best gets you the best results — much better than the results other people get who aren't willing to pay . . . or who can't pay.

Is it fair? No. But it's the truth.

CHAPTER

13

Use of Samples

> *"The product itself should be its own best salesman," says Hopkins to begin this chapter. "Not the product alone, but the product plus a mental impression, and atmosphere, which you place around it."*

Those are the key words: **"the mental impression and atmosphere"** you place around what you are selling.

Now you may be tempted to think Hopkins is simply talking about offering your prospect a sample of your product — such as the nice lady who hands out fresh baked cookies at the grocery store.

You'd only be partly correct.

Yes, Hopkins mentions "clothing," "phonograph records," and other examples.

But what he is really talking about are **PREMIUMS** and **FREEMIUMS.**

For example: "Request our FREE booklet *How to Write Effective Sales Letters* and we'll also send you another FREE booklet *How to Write Effective Postcards*."

In that example, the postcards booklet is the freemium. If you had to buy the sales letter book, then the extra free book you get is called a premium.

Let's let Hopkins continue:

"Samples serve numerous valuable purposes. They enable one to use the word FREE in ads. That often multiplies the readers. Most people want to learn about any offered gift. Tests often show that samples pay for themselves — perhaps several times over — in multiplying the readers of your ads without additional cost of space.

"A sample gets action. The reader of your ad may not be convinced to the point of buying. But he is ready to learn more about the product that you offer. So he cuts out a coupon, lays it aside, and later mails it or presents it. Without that coupon he would soon forget.

"Then you have the name and address of an interested prospect. You can start him using your product. You can give him fuller information. You can follow him up.

"That reader might not again read one of your ads in six months. Your impression would be lost. But when he writes you, you have a chance to complete with that prospect all that can be done. In that saving of waste the sample pays for itself."

It's amazing that these words were written way back in the 1920s, and they still apply to today's digital marketing age.

And it's another reason why lead generation advertising and direct response marketing are so effective in getting you the customers and clients you want.

Because you know exactly where to FOLLOW UP. And so many marketers give up too soon.

I can show you how to target your prospect, get those interested to reveal themselves, and then use the bulk of your marketing budget to sell to those who have already shown interest.

"Another way in which samples pay is by keying your advertisements," continues Hopkins. "They register the interest you create. Thus you can compare one with another ad, headline, plan and method. That means in any line an enormous saving. The wisest, most experienced man cannot tell what will most appeal in any line of copy. Without a key to guide you, your returns are very apt to cost you twice what they need cost. And we know that some ads on the same product will cost ten times what others cost. A sample may pay for itself several times over by giving you an accurate check."

Remember, you are the one courting the prospect. Don't make it difficult for them to respond to you. An inquiry means that a prospect has read your story and is interested. He or she would like to try your product and learn more about it. Do what you would do if that prospect stood before you.

Hopkins ends the chapter by being **DIRECT** about how to offer premiums and freemiums:

"Give them only to people to whom you have told your story. First create an atmosphere of respect, a desire, an expectation. When people are in that mood, your sample will usually confirm the qualities you claim... Here again comes the advantage of figuring cost per customer. That is the only way to gauge advertising. Samples sometimes seem to double advertising cost. They often cost more than the advertising. Yet, rightly used, they almost invariably form the cheapest way to get customers. And that is what you want."

Yes, indeed. That is exactly what you want.

And that is exactly what I can help you get.

CHAPTER

14

Getting Distribution

Chapter Fourteen of Scientific Advertising may seem out of date, at least, on the surface. Don't let that stop you from learning from it.

H**opkins begins with a statement that is still true today:**

"Most advertisers are confronted with the problem of getting distribution. National advertising is unthinkable without that. A venture cannot be profitable if nine in ten of the converts fail to find the goods."

No argument there from me. And I continue to nod my head YES as he makes other points:

- To force dealers to stock by bringing repeated demands may be enormously expensive.

- To cover the country with a selling force is usually impossible.

- To get dealers to stock an unknown line on promise of advertising is not easy. They have seen too many efforts fail, too many promises rescinded.

And then he gets to the real crux of the matter, with this advice:

"Start by soliciting direct sales — mail orders — until the volume of demand forces dealers to supply... Some get into touch with prospects by a sample or other offer, then refer them to certain dealers who are stocked."

Today, we have a lot of things that didn't exist back during Claude Hopkins' time — such as the Internet and shopping malls.

But if he was here, I bet he'd give this advice:

BE CAREFUL DRIVING PROSPECTS TO THE INTERNET.

Why?

Because the Internet is one big vast shopping mall ripe for comparing and contrasting you versus all of your competitors.

The truth is, you want to sell to your prospect in a vacuum.

Why would you want to drive your prospect to your website where they can easily click over to your competitor's website and get your marketing messages all jumbled up?

Think of it like this:

If you are selling shoes, which is better — a prospect coming directly to you for the specific shoe you sell…

…Or the prospect going to the mall to "shop for shoes"?

Perhaps there are 12 different shoe stores in the mall. The prospect comes to your store. Sees a pair of shoes they like. They are almost ready to buy. But wait, they think, let me go see if I can find something I like better... cheaper, etc.

These are not good odds for YOU, the seller.

But if you have previously targeted that prospect, pre-sold them on wanting your shoes, gave them an incentive to come into your shoe store at the mall...

...You have then invalidated all of your competition.

It is then irrelevant if there are 12 other shoe stores in the same mall with you.

The prospect wants YOUR shoes from YOUR store. And they will come directly to you to get it.

That is the power of direct marketing. That is the power of selling in a vacuum.

When you drive your prospect to the Internet, you put the sale at risk.

The secret strategy that successful direct marketers use is to keep the prospect off-line... with printed materials — direct mail, catalogs, sales literature, information kits, and other direct response marketing collateral.

"Some of the most successful advertisers have done this in a national way," says Hopkins. "They have inserted coupon ads in magazines, each coupon good at any store for a full-size package."

He, of course, wasn't talking about the Internet or shopping malls, but his points are still valid.

He continues:

"In these ways, many advertisers get national distribution without employing a single salesman. They get it immediately. And they get it at far lower cost than by any other method... But don't start advertising without distribution. Don't get distribution by methods too expensive. Or by slow, old-fashioned methods. The loss of time may cost you enormously in sales. And it may enable energetic rivals to get ahead of you."

And Hopkins ends the chapter with advice I feel best points to what I want to do for you when he says, "Go to those who know by countless experiences the best plan to apply to your line."

Regardless of what you sell, I can help you sell more. I can help you find more prospects. And I can help you save money, eliminate marketing waste, and get the results you want.

CHAPTER

15

Test Campaigns

"When a certain method has proved itself profitable I hesitate to drop it, until I have found and proved a better method by some local tests. The best way found to sell a product to thousands is probably the best way to sell other thousands."

Heed this advice from Claude Hopkins:

"Almost any question can be answered, cheaply, quickly and finally, by a test campaign. And that's the way to answer them — not by arguments around a table. Go to the court of last resort — the buyers of your product."

One of the biggest mistakes I see wannabe direct marketers make is diving into a campaign without testing.

You think you know how to sell your product profitably; your staff thinks they know how; your advertising agency thinks they know.

But they don't.

The only ones who *really* know are your prospects in the marketplace.

You probably believe your product or service is better than your competitors. But it could take a lot of money to move the marketplace in your direction.

"In the old days, advertisers ventured on their own opinions," Hopkins tells us in Chapter Fifteen. "The few guessed right, the many wrong. Those were the times of advertising disasters. Even those who succeeded came close to the verge before the tide was turned. They did not know their cost per customer or their sale per customer. The cost of selling might take long to come back. Often it never came back."

This is exactly what I try to avoid for my clients. As Claude Hopkins put it:

"We let the thousands decide what the millions will do. We make a small venture and watch cost and result. When we learn what a thousand customers cost, we know almost exactly what a million will cost. When we learn what they buy, we know what a million will buy.

"We establish averages on a small scale, and those averages always hold. We know our cost, we know our sale, we know our profit or our loss. We know how soon our cost comes back. Before we spread out, we prove our undertaking absolutely safe. So there are today no advertising disasters piloted by men who know."

Let's just say that you have a list universe of 25,000 prospects, and you want to send a package promoting your service.

The worst thing you could do is mail to all 25,000 at once.

Think about everything I've talked about in this book up to this point. You don't really know how the market is going to respond. You don't really know if the market prefers:

- Soft offer, hard offer, negative offer, or deferred offer
- Free trial, free gift, or free shipping
- Long-term guarantee, money-back guarantee, buy-back guarantee
- Group discount, relationship discount, quantity discount
- Limited editions, premium offers, deluxe versions

And on and on.

You haven't tested formats, teasers, headlines, copy blocks, calls to action, and other selling points.

The truth is, you really don't *know* what's going to work best.

"Sometimes we find that the cost of the advertising comes back before the bills are due," writes Hopkins. "That means that the product can be advertised without investment. Many a great advertiser has been built up without any cost whatever beyond immediate receipts. That is an ideal situation."

That's why I suggest you take a portion of your list — perhaps 15 to 20 percent — and test.

From a few thousand, you can learn what tens of thousands will do. I'll help you discover your winners.

"In five years for one food advertiser we tried out over fifty separate plans. Every little while we found an improvement, so the results of our advertising constantly grew. At the end of five years we found the best plan of all. It reduced our cost of selling by 75 percent.

"That is what mail order advertisers do — try out plan after plan to constantly reduce the cost."

During Hopkins' day, and during this current age, we direct response marketers test… and test… and test.

Until we develop for you a direct response marketing machine that works every time in your favor.

If your advertising agency or your brand shop or your marketing staff are not doing this for you, your big question should be "Why?"

How do they know that what they are doing for you is the absolute best thing that can be done?

The answer is, they don't know. They're guessing. With your money. As long as you'll keep spending, they'll keep taking.

I want you to know… *and know you know.*

CHAPTER

16

Leaning on Dealers

It's surprising how little has changed from Hopkins' day. He gives some good advice on "Leaning on Dealers" in Chapter Sixteen. Here are some of the highlights:

We cannot depend much in most lines on the active help of dealers. They are busy.

The average dealer exerts himself on brands of his own, if at all.

Making a sale without making a convert does not count for much. Sales made by conviction — by advertising — are likely to bring permanent customers. People who buy through casual recommendations do not often stick. Next time someone else gives other advice.

That last point deserves to be repeated: making a sale without making a convert does not count for much.

You are looking for long-term results. You want lifetime value from your customer.

Here are some other important points from Hopkins:

Much money is often frittered away on other forms of dealer help. Perhaps on window or store displays. A window display, acting as a reminder, may bring to one dealer a lion's share of the trade. Yet it may not increase your total sales at all.

Those are facts to find out. Try one town in one way, one in another. Compare total sales in those towns. In many lines such tests will show that costly displays are worthless. A growing number of experienced advertisers spend no money on displays.

We put things to the test. We compare cost and result on every form of expenditure. It is easily done. Very many costly wastes are eliminated by this modern process.

Scientific advertising has altered many old plans and conceptions. It has proved many long-established methods to be folly. And why should we not apply to these things the same criteria we apply to other forms of selling? Or to manufacturing costs?

Your object in all advertising is to buy new customers at a price which pays a profit... Learn what your consumers cost and what they buy. If they cost you one dollar each, figure that every wasted dollar costs you a possible customer.

Your business will be built in that way, not by dealer help. You must do your own selling, make your own success. Be content if dealers fill the orders that you bring. Eliminate your wastes.

Spend all your ammunition where it counts most.

I believe — and have proven time and time again — that your best ammunition is direct response marketing.

It's how you test... how you prove... how you know... and how you get the results you want.

Ideally, it starts with the market. What do they want? Why do they want it? What have they done in the past to get it? Why are they not satisfied with their previous efforts?

The more your message can make your market want what you've got, the more they will pay for it.

However, the hungry prospect who wants what you sell will probably still resist you multiple times. That's why you need a lead generation campaign to capture interested prospects and follow up for as long as it takes.

Don't expect a dealer to do that for you.

Use whatever media — and hopefully a combination of media — to keep delivering your messages.

Keep nurturing your leads as they come in. You need messages for cold prospects; different messages for hot leads, and different messages for those growing cold again.

Your goal should be to make the sale so that you can make a customer for life.

CHAPTER
17
Individuality

The next time your advertising agency wants you to do something "creative"... something "edgy"... something to create some "buzz"... remember what Claude Hopkins teaches in this chapter:

"**A person who desires to make an impression must stand out in some way from the masses. And in a pleasing way,**" says Hopkins.

"Being eccentric, being abnormal is not a distinction to covet. But doing admirable things in a different way gives one a great advantage."

The same can be said of marketing. Uniqueness can sometimes arouse interest or provoke resentment.

Hopkins explains:

"We try to give each advertiser a becoming style. We make him distinctive, perhaps not in appearance, but in manner and in tone. He is given an individuality best suited to the people he addresses.

"One man appears rugged and honest in a line where rugged honesty counts. One may be a good fellow where choice is a matter of favor. In other lines the man stands out by impressing himself as an authority."

Others have explored the weapons of influences used by marketers. Most notably, Dr. Robert Cialdini chronicled them in his book *Influence: The Psychology of Persuasion*. He categorized them as:

- Reciprocation
- Commitment
- Consistency
- Social Proof
- Liking
- Authority
- Scarcity

Cialdini wrote of these in the 1980s, but Hopkins was writing about weapons of influence in the 1920s.

"Whenever possible we introduce a personality into our ads," writes Hopkins. "By making a man famous we make his product famous. When we claim an improvement, naming the man who made it adds effect… We don't want people to think that salesmanship is made to order. That our appeals are created, studied, artificial. They must seem to come from the heart… There are winning personalities in ads as well as people. To some we are glad to listen, others bore us. Some are refreshing, some commonplace. Some inspire confidence, some caution.

"To create the right individuality is a supreme accomplishment. Then an advertiser's growing reputation on that line brings him ever-increasing prestige. Never weary of that part. Remember that a change in our characteristics would compel our best friends to get acquainted all over."

That's why I advise my clients to stick to their winners — and keep trying to beat them.

But never get tired of your winners.

You see your marketing and advertising for your company every day. You live it and breathe it… and you probably get sick of it.

You might make the mistake of thinking others are getting sick of it, too.

That is almost never the case.

You will get bored with your direct marketing far quicker than the marketplace will. Let **them** tell you when they are bored by their reaction — namely, not buying.

Hold fast to that which is working.

And hold every piece of marketing accountable for its results.

CHAPTER

18

Negative Advertising

If there is one chapter I don't completely agree with, it's this one. I bet you can think of dozens perhaps hundreds of examples where negative advertising persuaded millions of people to action. But let's allow Hopkins to have his say. Here is Chapter Eighteen in its entirety:

To attack a rival is never good advertising. Don't point out others' faults. It is not permitted in the best mediums. It is never good policy. The selfish purpose is apparent. It looks unfair, not sporting. If you abhor knockers, always appear a good fellow.

Show the bright side, the happy and attractive side, not the dark and uninviting side of things.

Show beauty, not homeliness; health, not sickness. Don't show the wrinkles you propose to remove, but the face as it will appear. Your customers know all about the wrinkles.

In advertising a dentifrice, show pretty teeth, not bad teeth. Talk of coming good conditions, not conditions which exist. In advertising clothes, picture well-dressed people, not the shabby.

Picture successful men, not failures, when you advertise a business course. Picture what others wish to be, not what they may be now.

We are attracted by sunshine, beauty, happiness, health, success. Then point the way to them, not the way out of the opposite.

Picture envied people, not the envious. Tell people what to do, not what to avoid.

Make your every ad breathe good cheer. We always dodge a Lugubrious Blue.

Assume that people will do what you ask. Say, "Send now for this sample." Don't say, "Why do you neglect this offer?" That suggests that people are neglecting. Invite them to follow the crowd.

Compare the results of two ads, one negative, one positive. One presenting the dark side, one the bright side. One warning, the other inviting. You will be surprised. You will find that the positive ad outpulls the other four to one, if you have our experience.

The "Before and after taking" ads are follies of the past. They never had a place save with the afflicted. Never let their memory lead you to picture the gloomy side of things.

CHAPTER

19

Letter Writing

Here is the bellwether of direct mail — the sales letter. At first, Hopkins states what seems obvious:

"Most of them go direct to the waste basket... others are filed for reference."

But the crux of the matter is why? Why does one letter succeed while another fails?

"The ones you act on or the ones you keep have a headline which attracted your interest. At a glance they offer something that you want, something you may wish to know. Remember that point in all advertising."

The point is, letter writers often fail to get the right attention. They fail to tell what buyers wish to know.

One magazine sends out millions of letters annually. Some to get subscriptions, some to sell books. Before the publisher sends out five million letters, he puts a few thousands to test. He may try twenty-five letters, each with a thousand prospects. He learns what results will cost.

The letter which pays best is the letter that is used.

"Mail order advertisers do likewise," says Hopkins. "They test their letters as they test their ads... where that is not possible, they should be based on knowledge gained by tests. We find the same difference in letters as in ads. Some get action, some do not. Some complete a sale, some forfeit the impression gained. These letters, going usually to half-made converts, are tremendously important."

It will come to no surprise to you that Hopkins rightly believes a letter which goes to an inquirer is like a salesperson going to an interested prospect. You know what created that interest. Then follow it up along that line, not on some different argument.

Complete the impression already created. Don't undertake another on a guess.

"In a letter as in ads, the great point is to get immediate action," Hopkins tells us. "People are naturally dilatory. They postpone, and a postponed action is too often forgotten.

"Do something if possible to get immediate action. Offer some inducement for it. Or tell what delay may cost. Note how many successful selling letters place a limit on an offer. It expires on a certain date. That is all done to get a prompt decision, to overcome the tendency to delay."

There are many ways to capture attention, communicate your message, and persuade your audience to action. Regardless of which you use, "strike while the iron is hot" as Hopkins would say. Get a decision. Have it followed by prompt action when you can.

One of the ways you can make your sales letters more effective is to use the AIDA formula. It's been around for a long time — for a reason. It works. And most of the "new" and "proprietary" formulas out there nowadays are just blatant rip-offs of AIDA... old wine in new bottles.

AIDA stands for:

- *Attention* — get it with a strong teaser, headline, and opening paragraph.

- *Interest* — pique it by appealing to the reader's problems, needs, and wants.

- *Desire* — create demand by offering the benefits of your product or service.

- *Action* — persuade your reader to take the next step.

One of the best ways to capture and hold someone's imagination is to promise to solve a problem they are currently dealing with.

The reader isn't interested in you. The reader is interested in the reader.

So make your letter all about them and create a desire for what you are offering. Hook the reader's interest.

And your letters will get better results.

CHAPTER

20

A Name That Helps

Chapter Twenty of Scientific Advertising — with its products of yesteryear — is a charming time capsule of marketing from the 1920s. Yet, if you don't allow the antiquated language to fool you, there is a lot of wisdom here.

There is great advantage in a name that tells a story. The name is usually prominently displayed.

To justify the space it occupies, it should aid the advertising. Some such names are almost complete advertisements in themselves. May Breath is such a name. Cream of Wheat is another.

That name alone has been worth a fortune. Other examples are Dutch Cleanser, Cuticura, Dyanshine, Minute Tapioca, 3-in-One Oil, Holeproof, Alcorub, etc.

Such names may be protected, yet the name itself describes the product, so it makes a valuable display.

Other coined names are meaningless. Some examples are Kodak, Karo, Mazda, Sapolio, Vaseline, Kotex, Lux, Postum, etc. They can be protected, and long-continued advertising may give them a meaning. When this is accomplished, they become very valuable. But the great majority of them never attain that status.

Such names do not aid the advertising. It is very doubtful if they justify display. The service of the product, not the name, is the important thing in advertising. A vast amount of space is wasted in displaying names and pictures which tell no selling story. The tendency of modern advertising is to eliminate this waste.

Other coined names signify ingredients which anyone may use.

Examples are Syrup of Figs, Coconut Oil Shampoo, Tar Soap, Palmolive Soap, etc.

Such products may dominate a market if the price is reasonable, but they must to a degree meet competition. They invite substitution. They are naturally classified with other products which have like ingredients, so the price must remain in that class.

Toasted Corn Flakes and Malted Milk are examples of unfortunate names. In each of those cases one advertiser created a new demand. When the demand was created, others shared it because they could use the name. The originators depended only on a brand. It is interesting to speculate on how much more profitable a coined name might have been.

On a patented product it must be remembered that the right to a name expires with the patent.

Names like Castoria, Aspirin, Shredded Wheat Biscuit, etc., have become common property. This is a very serious point to consider. It often makes a patent an undesirable protection.

Another serious fault in coined names is frivolity. In seeking uniqueness one gets something trivial. And that is a fatal handicap in a serious product. It almost prohibits respect.

When a product must be called by a common name, the best auxiliary name is a man's name. It is much better than a coined name, for it shows that some man is proud of his creation.

Thus the question of a name is of serious importance in laying the foundations of a new undertaking. Some names have become the chief factors in success. Some have lost for their originators four-fifths of the trade they developed.

CHAPTER

21

Good Business

In the final chapter of Scientific Advertising, Claude Hopkins starts off by getting personal.

If a thing is useful they call it work, if useless they call it play. One is as hard as the other. One can be just as much a game as the other. In both there is rivalry. There's a struggle to excel the rest. All the difference I see lies in attitude of mind.

"A rapid stream ran by the writer's boyhood home. The stream turned a wooden wheel and the wheel ran a mill. Under that primitive method, all but a fraction of the stream's potentiality went to waste.

"Then someone applied scientific methods to that stream — put in a turbine and dynamos. Now, with no more water, no more power, it runs a large manufacturing plant.

"We think of that stream when we see wasted advertising power. And we see it everywhere — hundreds of examples. Enormous potentialities — millions of circulation — used to turn a mill wheel. While others use that same power with manifold effect.

"We see countless ads running year after year which we know to be unprofitable. Men spending five dollars to do what one dollar might do. Men getting back 30 percent of their cost when they might get 150 percent. And the facts could be easily proved.

"We see wasted space, frivolity, clever conceits, entertainment. Costly pages filled with palaver which, if employed by a salesman, would reflect on his sanity. But those ads are always unkeyed. The money is spent blindly, merely to satisfy some advertising whim.

"Not new advertisers only. Many an old advertiser has little or no idea of his advertising results. The business is growing through many efforts combined, and advertising is given its share of the credit."

Then, Hopkins issues this challenge:

"End an ad with an offer to pay five dollars to anyone who writes you that he read the ad through. The scarcity of replies will amaze you."

"Replies" are exactly what I'm determined to get for you. Replies in response, by phones calls, by checks in the mail, by visits to your website, by customers in your store, whatever the call to action you want.

I can help you win on the small scale, so you can roll your direct response marketing out on a large scale — and win even bigger.

You don't have to be a marketing victim ever again.

You **CAN** know — like a well-oiled machine — that the marketing you produce will work for you, make you a profit, and get you the results you want.

Every piece of marketing you implement — print, broadcast, internet, sales collateral — must justify its cost for you.

"Yet most national advertising is done without justification," Hopkins would say. "It is merely presumed to pay. A little test might show a way to multiply returns."

Hopkins ends *Scientific Advertising* with these final thoughts:

"The time is fast coming when men who spend money are going to know what they get. Good business and efficiency will be applied to advertising. Men and methods will be measured by the known returns, and only competent men can survive… And we shall be prouder of it when we are judged on merit."

EPILOGUE

The Jay Huling Way

You have come to a crossroads with your marketing.

You can either go one direction... and get results.

Or go another direction... and not get results.

The choice is yours.

The Huling Way is the way of results.

I realize one of the reasons you've read my book is because you want to know more about how you can have better marketing, get better results, make more money, and stop wasting money on marketing that doesn't work.

But at some point, you're going to want to know more about me. If you've reached that level of interest, this is my chance to grandstand.

You asked for it, so here are 10 points I believe you need to know about me:

I've been a marketing consultant and copywriter since 1988. I specialize in direct response — direct mail, email marketing, print campaigns, websites, radio and TV, and sales collateral.

Over the years, my clients have included a lot of big names — such as: AAA, AARP, Aflac, American Lung Association, Atlantic Marine, AVIS Rent-a-Car, Barnett Banks, Blue Cross Blue Shield, Cigna Health, Citibank, Crowley Maritime Corporation, CSX Transportation, E! Entertainment Television, Environmental Protection Agency, EverBank, First Union, Habitat for Humanity, Horace Mann, MLB Network, Physicians Mutual, Pitney Bowes, Royal Caribbean, Salvation Army, U.S. Army Corps of Engineers, USO, Vistakon, Wounded Warrior Project.

And I've also created a lot of successful winning campaigns for smaller companies you may not have heard of — such as: American Resort Specialty Services, Arthur Treacher's Seafood Grille, Ethan Allen, First Florida Credit Union, Gainesville Health & Fitness, GATE Petroleum, Hospitality Marketing Concepts, New York Vacation Club, Peterbrooke Chocolatier, Regency Centers, St. Vincent's Health Systems, Web.com, X-Force Body.

I am under several non-disclosure contracts by advertising agencies, brand shops, direct mail houses, and lettershops to write for their clients — without their clients knowing about it. So, I can't tell you who they are. I may have even written for you already, and you aren't aware of it — if your agency secretly hired me to write it.

To the best of my knowledge, all of these current agencies are the good ones: the ones not trying to rip you off.

A lot of my work has won numerous industry awards — like: Addy, AME, AVA, ECHO, Effie, MarCom, MAXI, OBIE, PRSA, Silver Microphone, Stevie, Summit EMA, and Telly. I even won Best of Category at the International Wildlife Film Festival. But don't let any of that impress you. As we talked about earlier, a lot of those awards are high-priced beauty contests or trophy mills. None of it really matters. The only thing that matters is the results I get for you.

And I've gotten my clients a lot of results. Some examples: A few years ago, a non-profit client ask me to write a direct mail fundraising package that would raise them at least $50,000. I wrote it; they mailed it, and it raised more than $450,000 on its first drop. Another non-profit raised more than $1.2 million with a campaign of mine. And yet another for a church raised more than $4 million.

When you hire me and we work together, your input and collaboration are welcome — but I make the final decisions. I offer a money-back guarantee on my work — which goes like this: "If you implement what I craft for you, I personally guarantee you will find business, get business, and keep business within 39 days. If you don't, let me know and I'll issue a prompt and courteous refund of the copywriting fees you paid me." I can't guarantee your ideas, only mine. There are reasons behind the strategy, copy, and consultation I provide for you. We will agree in advance that your participation is limited.

I prefer to work with results-oriented clients. Getting results for you is the only thing I care about. I don't even care if you like what I create for you. I might not like it either. But if it's going to get results for you, that's what we're going to use. Of course, if you pay me enough, I am always willing to make exceptions.

I make no apologies for my high fees. I have earned the right to charge them. I'm not the way you lower your marketing costs. I'm the way you make money. You are paying me so that you can have a winning horse in the race.

I will show you how to build a powerful direct marketing campaign, so you can attract satisfied customers, clients, patients, or donors — guaranteed or your money back — even if you've been previously burned by advertising charlatans and marketing guru wannabes (or just by an incompetent staff.)

And here's a bonus point:

I believe my marketing newsletter THE HULING LETTER is the best free monthly newsletter mailed in the United States. This is a real newsletter delivered by the post office, not some annoying e-zine. If you are not a subscriber, you should be. Request your free subscription by sending me an email to jay@jayhuling.com.

The Jay Huling direct response marketing way:

- Gains attention
- Focuses on the customer
- Stresses benefits
- Differentiates you from the competition
- Proves its case
- Establishes credibility
- Builds value
- Closes with a call to action

Always remember that your prospect seeks advantages, improvements, and new ways to satisfy desires — whether it is personal or business.

The Huling Way is to **sell** — sometimes with a story, sometimes with facts, but always with what the reader wants to know.

When we work together, I will transfer all my years of experience and knowledge to your project... to fight for you... to sell for you... to win for you.

Yes, you will win.

WHAT THEY SAY ABOUT JAY

Jay Learned From the Best

"I was good friends with the legendary copywriter and filmmaker Herschell Gordon Lewis, and we hired him a lot until he passed away in 2016. When I first saw Jay's copy in action, I thought it was Herschell's because the sales arguments had the same compelling, emotional, and irresistible sense of urgency. Then I learned Jay was a fan and student of Herschell's, and it all made sense. You see it in Jay's work for clients such as AAA, AARP, Aflac, Cigna, Citibank, Physicians Mutual, and others. He makes the sales messages jump off the page and practically forces the reader to take action. That's what Herschell called the art of writing copy, and Jay has mastered it well. If we could be blessed to still have Herschell Gordon Lewis with us today, I'm sure he'd recommend Jay Huling, too."

Cindy Dunhill
Vice President — Operations, Dunhill International List Company, Inc.

Jay's Copy is to the Point, Smooth, and Persuasive

"Jay has the ability to delve deep inside the minds of people, connect with their wants, and stimulate a desire to fulfill those needs with your product or service. I love his work for our catalog and other marketing because Jay does a wonderful job of combining specifics with romance to induce a smile and a purchase. So, if you are looking for an accomplished copywriter — capable and creative — who develops selling arguments that hold your readers from start to finish, I recommend you hire Jay Huling. You will transform your marketing from dull to dazzling."

Phyllis Lockwood Geiger
Founder, Peterbrooke Chocolatier

Jay Is On the Side of the Entrepreneur

"I know a lot of business owners and entrepreneurs because I am one of them. The struggles are real, even when the economy is going well — worse when it's not. The entrepreneur is a risk-taker who often must worry about market conditions, competition, taxes, rising costs, or the monthly need to pay debt and make payroll. No smart marketer has the funds to waste money on advertising. That's why I've always admired Jay's approach to using marketing to make his clients money. His work has always worked for me. He likes to say he is just a salesman in print, but I will take it further than that: Jay is a master closer in print. He's a kindred spirit to the business owner, and you don't have to take my word for it; just get a hold of some of his direct mail and see for yourself."

Ralph Pressley, CMA
Chief Financial Officer, Marathon Equity

I'm Impressed with the Way Jay Gets Things Done

"I first met Jay on the set of some TV commercials we were working on, and the shoot wasn't going so well when he first showed up. I thought — oh, no — the scriptwriter is here to stick his nose into production. Just what we need. I've seen these kinds of guys before, and they just get in the way. But everyone seemed to like Jay. He does have a unique charm and a great sense of humor and a way to disarm every situation with his wit. So, I gave him a chance, and we got along well. Jay would talk to the actors, the director, the client; he was just kind of there. You never noticed Jay trying to influence, but I would notice the actors started doing things more the way Jay wanted; the director started directing Jay's way; the client became more agreeable to everything, and no one seemed to realize it. And that's when I realized Jay is an evil genius. His charm and wit disguised everything, but he was manipulating the entire process. He was the Alpha Dog blending into the scenery — the kind of guy who

makes you think the good ideas are yours, when they are really his. The same thing happened when Jay showed up for post-production. He sat next to me chatting and making jokes as I edited the spots, occasionally commenting on what I was doing. Afterwards, I realized I had done everything he wanted without knowing. I asked him about it later, and he just chalked it up to verbal control and equivoque. I didn't know whether to believe him or not — but with every project we work on, I'm always impressed with the way Jay gets things done."

Randy Bernhardt
President, PostOp, Inc.

Jay Creates Marketing Assets That You Can Use Again and Again

"Before I hired him, I was told about Jay's reputation as a results-driven direct response strategist. He's earned it, and he didn't disappoint, but he did surprise me. I just wanted Jay to write my letter, but he was focused on my list at first. Then he convinced me to increase my offer. And then he lectured me about being dedicated to follow-up marketing. If that wasn't enough, he continued to preach market segmentation and converting warm leads into hot prospects. Yes, this can be frustrating at first when you just want a letter written. But to Jay's credit, all his meddling turned our simple letters into lead generation assets. Now, we can take a letter Jay wrote for us, tweak it a little to match a new market segment, send it out and get good results — time and time again. Plus, he's a class act to work with. But even if he wasn't, he'd be worth it in ROI and all the advice he gives."

Thomas C. Keller
Managing Principal, Keller Partners & Company

Jay Wants to Inspire Others to Help Non-Profits

"While I served on the board of Wounded Warrior Project, I appreciated Jay's desire to help tell the stories of our injured service members. Not only did he write articles about me and my fellow veterans, but he also helped our communications team with marketing materials, fundraising, and script writing. Perhaps most people know him for his direct response marketing campaigns, but I feel it is his ability to tell a compelling story — especially for non-profits — that is Jay's real passion."

Dawn Halfaker
Owner and CEO, Halfaker and Associates
Director, Board of Directors, Wounded Warrior Project (2007 – 2015)

Jay Is A Lot of Fun to Work With

"I always prefer to work with successful people who are accomplished in their craft. Jay is one of those people. Yes, his availability can be frustrating because he often has clients on a waiting list. So, I know I probably can't rely on Jay for a rush project. But he is an expert, a professional, and a trusted advisor when it comes to marketing. I admire how he believes in a science-based system for creating copy that produces desired results. Plus, he is a lot of fun to work with. When I would read the scripts for the video blogs Jay wrote for me, my reaction was often, "Only Jay would have thought of that."

Illiana Stoilova
Co-Founder, X-Force Body

Jay Will Earn Your Respect

"If you are going to hire Jay as your marketing consultant, be prepared to have your beliefs challenged. He's going to question everything, but I like that — because he practices what my favorite author Napoleon Hill classified as the Principle of Accurate Thinking. He wants the marketing

messages he creates for you to be true and relevant to the needs and desires of your prospects. If you are looking for a yes-man, look elsewhere. There is a science, reason, principle, and history behind the copy and advice that Jay provides — and he's not shy about sharing it with you. And he has a great sense of humor - a sign of creativity to me. He's a little more expensive than others, but marketing requires a highly skilled professional. The most important element to me is producing results and Jay does that."

Joe Cirulli
Owner and CEO, Gainesville Health & Fitness

You Can Hire Better Copywriters Than Jay Huling

"If you have the money, hire one of those superstar marketers like Dan Kennedy, Clayton Makepeace, John Carlton, or Bob Bly, and be prepared to pay $100,000 or more. Yes, Jay's fees are high, but they're not that high; although, he might match those guys in ego. Jay actually earns his living writing and creating campaigns for clients — not selling books, giving speeches, conducting seminars, or hosting super conferences. I've worked on numerous projects with Jay, and I've always been glad he was on the job. When a client has a question, Jay will not only have the answer, but also the history, science, and track record of the answer. Sometimes it's an unwanted education he heaps on the client. But it is always a demonstration of his expertise and credibility. So, if you have to put up with some of Jay's marketing eccentricities along the way, I suggest you do it. Because he's going to get you the ROI you'd get from those superstars at a fraction of the cost."

Mark A. Esbeck
President, Andrick & Associates

Jay is the Best in the Business

"My first impression of Jay didn't go so well. I initially asked for a meeting to discuss potentially hiring him for an upcoming project. Jay agreed, but he informed me he charged for consultations. I thought he was joking. No one ever charged us for consultations. Advertising agencies even do spec creative at no charge. Who did Jay think he was, I asked. But Jay assured me the fee would be refunded from the final invoice if he was hired for the project. So, reluctantly, I agreed. That was the last time I doubted Jay. There are very few real marketing savants in this business. Jay is one of them. His direct mail packages have generated countless profits for a variety of clients. I've been repeatedly impressed by his unique ability to generate clear, compelling, persuasive copy. I admit — I'm never happy about Jay's high fees, but I'm never disappointed by the results."

Michael K. Houpt
Cruise Director/Production Manager, Royal Caribbean International

Jay Can Help Your Business Succeed and Fulfill Your Purpose

"Jay can be peculiar to work with and sometimes quite the contradiction. The first drafts of his direct response copywriting for us can often be too salesy; while his radio commercial scriptwriting can be a little too avant-garde. But what's great about Jay is that he's willing to adjust his copy to fit the client's corporate comfort level. He's also not shy about telling you exactly what his strategy is, while backing up his opinions with historical precedent from previous campaigns. And I admire that. I admit Jay's fees can seem high, but I don't know any entrepreneur who wants their marketing in the hands of amateurs. I've always enjoyed working with Jay, and when there is a

project that fits his skills, I know he's a critical thinker who will put the best interest of our needs over his creative tendencies."

Michelle Troha
Senior Vice President Marketing, First Florida Credit Union

Jay Offers Powerful Copy and Marketing Strategy

"Jay is well-known for the selling power of his copy. However, it's the marketing ideas and strategies that help his clients the most. Even the free ideas he gives away every month in his newsletter can result in big improvements in a company's revenues and bottom line — if they will simply implement his suggestions. He's spent more than 30 years developing this knowledge. All you have to do is ask him to transfer his proven techniques from his mind into yours."

Teddy Solomon
CEO, ATC Broadband

Jay Has a Tendency to Be Too Verbose

"Jay is one of the students of the great masters of direct response copywriting such as Claude Hopkins, John Caples, and David Ogilvy. So he is very agile with long copy. Good luck getting him to write 'Hello' in less than 500 words. Now, granted, he does a lot of work in health, finance, and insurance, as well as tourism, and those markets need longer copy. So if you are in an industry where you need a long-winded, long-copy guy who will write until he runs out of benefits and lets the message tell him how long it should be, Jay is the copywriter for you."

Peter Gorla
Vice President & Chief Marketing Officer,
Hospitality Marketing Concepts, VOILA Hotel Rewards

Make Sure You Know What You're Getting Into When You Hire Jay

"I've worked a lot with Jay and his clients, and I've even hired him to work with some of mine. His work stands out because it is often so counterintuitive, so different, so outrageous. I've worked with him on scripts where a client expected a straightforward talking-head video, but Jay had them perform magic tricks, talk with puppets, react to green screen footage of King Kong attacking them, and even go topless. Sometimes the clients are initially a little wary of Jay's ideas. But when they see how outrageously successful the final product becomes, they are all too happy to cash the checks his methods of madness produce. I encourage you to hire Jay — if you dare."

Steve McMillan
Owner/Director of Photography, Advantage Video Production

Expect the Unexpected from Jay

"Art directors and copywriters often get along about as well as Road Runner and Wile E. Coyote. But I've never felt like detonating a big Acme bomb over Jay's copy. In fact, I've always appreciated how easy he is to work with. He welcomes input and collaboration — but you can expect him to take responsibility for the final decisions. I admire how he examines the symptoms of his clients' marketing problems and then prescribes a specific course of action. If you're not an expert at marketing, you probably will be after a few months of talking with Jay. He will give you so many ideas you'll probably have trouble implementing them all. The techniques that he unleashes on you might have you using that Acme bomb to blow up your marketing and rethink your brand — but you'll be glad you did."

Phil Helow
Art Director, Helow Creative

Nobody Can Get Results Like Jay Can

"Jay Huling is by far the most talented and innovative copywriter I have ever had the privilege of working alongside. While his initial ideas sometimes seem out in left field, he has a unique and uncanny way of creating compelling campaigns, ranging from broadcast to direct response, that drive spectacular results. What's more - his copywriting and ideas always work and bring the client exactly what they are looking for. I have thoroughly enjoyed my years of working with Jay both remotely and in-person, and highly recommend him as a one-of-kind creative marketing mind whose work is unparalleled. He is a phenomenal asset to anyone looking to boost their business or is looking for extraordinary marketing."

Meghan Harding
Owner, MK Marketing & Media

Jay is the Real Deal

"Jay Huling is a writer's writer! I've known and worked with Jay for over 10 years and am constantly in awe of his command of not just writing, but communication. This guy gets it! I'm proud to have even the slightest connection to him through both my Florida Film & Tape (creative production company) and Blue Island Digital (digital media and advertising company). Always looking forward to the next collaboration."

Bradford Fuller
Creative Director, Florida Film & Tape, Blue Island Digital

I Never Thought I Could Afford Jay Huling

"I never thought I could afford to pay a marketing professional of Jay Huling's caliber to create a fundraising direct mail letter for our non-profit. Thankfully, my best friend knows Jay, and she convinced him to take on my project pro bono. I was so excited when I first read the letter Jay wrote for me that I could hardly contain myself. He is an invaluable resource that will help your fundraising appeals jump out and get noticed from the clutter of requests people get every day. I recommend you do yourself a favor and put Jay's expertise to work for you in the increasingly difficult fundraising environment. You'll be glad you did."

Charlene Phipps
Missionary Associate, Special Touch Ministry

Record-Breaking Direct Response Results

"Jay is truly the Babe Ruth of direct marketing. He seems to hit a homerun every time. When we tried it on our own, we used to run ads that ended up being just another line item on our expense sheet. There was not a return on the investment. But when we started running ads that Jay wrote, we saw a distinct increase in traffic to our locations. In fact, one of the ads Jay wrote for us broke the existing sales record for the Florida Times-Union and Jacksonville.com. His copy sold 437 hamburgers in less than 24 hours. His ideas, strategy, and advice have really helped take our business to the next level."

Kelly Harris
President & CEO, Times Grill

Jay Was the Difference Between Us Giving Up on the Project and Raising the Money We Needed

"I didn't understand the power of direct response sales copy until I met Jay Huling. Before consulting with Jay, we had tried everything we could to generate donations for a capital campaign project, and we were about to give up. Even after seeing the package Jay wrote for us, my first thought was this won't work. It's too much and no one is going to read all that, I argued. Jay guaranteed us it would work. He came highly recommended, and I knew he had a reputation and track record for generating results. So I made the decision to produce the package and drop it in the mail. If we were going down, we'd go down swinging. On the contrary, the results blew away my fears. We're so thankful because the package Jay developed for us paid off in droves. This was 2010, during one of the toughest economic times our country has seen in decades. We were able to generate a huge demand from people who wanted to get involved and help. My job became as simple as going to the mailbox every day and taking the donations mailed to the bank. Not only that, but we heard from one of our affluent parishioners who in the past we had tried to contact time and time again. We had never had any success with him until he got our package. He called, said he read the letter, and was willing to offer us a blank check for whatever we needed. That one campaign generated the most money ever in such a short amount of time. I was astounded how effortlessly Jay's campaign seemed to attract donors like a magnet."

Joe Chamberlain

Executive Director, Episcopal Diocese of Florida

Thanks for Getting Customers Into My Store

"A year ago, my business was completely flat lining. In fact, I wasn't even sure I'd be in business for very much longer. The institutional advertising Avis corporate provided my office simply wasn't working in my local market. I didn't need to build the Avis image. I needed to drive sales to my business. That's why I called you, and that is honestly the best business decision I'd made all year. The increased rentals and sales of insurance your work gave me made it worth every penny. As you know, I was skeptical at first because you wanted to do the exact opposite of what the local ad rep advised me to do. But you made a convincing case. I don't get a salary or an hourly wage. I earn my living solely from the cars I rent and the insurance I sell. So my advertising has to work. Thanks for getting customers into my store."

William Reeder
Owner/Operator, Avis Rent-a-Car

The Proof is in the Profits

Our profitability has quadrupled since we've been implementing Jay's advice. We're finally targeting the right prospects with our marketing. At first, we were worried that Jay's ideas were too radical, and quite frankly, too expensive. But the proof is in the profits and in the immediate results Jay has generated for us. I'm afraid to think how much money it would have cost us in failed marketing if we hadn't hired Jay. I would have never believed it unless I had experienced it for myself. And since our business is now more successful than ever, I can now take more time off and spend more time with my family — which is why we started our business in the first place."

Jan Campana
Owner & President, Dimples BBQ Sauce

What Changed My Mind Were the Results Jay Got for Me

"When I first hired Jay, I was thrilled with excitement for what it would mean for my business. He came well recommended, and I knew his impressive track record. However, when I first got the strategy plan and copy from him, I was horrified. I thought this simply wouldn't work for my business because we are so different, and Jay's ideas were unlike anything I had ever seen. Then I figured I would just use his work, wait out the 39 days, take advantage of his money-back guarantee, and ask for my money back. What changed my mind were the results Jay got for me. Calls kept coming in, excursions kept being booked, and the demand for our tours and services increased so much we had to raise our prices just to lower demand so we could handle it all. Needless to say, I never asked for my money back, and I continue to use Jay's coaching services to help use marketing to my greatest advantage."

Andres Lasota

Captain, Atlas Fun Boat, Barcelona Boat Charter

The Only Thing That's Worked for Me is Working with Jay

"When I first called Jay, I was desperate. I had tried other copywriters before. I had bought books, study courses, and had gone to marketing seminars. I had tried to implement things on my own, and nothing worked for me. What all the marketing, advertising, and branding gurus were promising and what they said others were experiencing was not happening for me. I didn't want to spend money on another expert and be disappointed again, but Jay was different. He preached a new way, and he practiced what he preached, and he showed me step-by-step how to make my marketing pay for itself so that I never really have to spend money on marketing. Now, as I implement Jay's techniques, I have the business I want, the income I want,

and the freedom from the feast or famine nightmares that plague so many entrepreneurs like me."

Pamela Burnett
Owner, DogVacay, Inc.

Jay is an Elite Copywriter and ROI Marketing Consultant

"In my humble opinion, the New York market has the best of the best of talent in terms of marketing and advertising professionals. So I was hesitant at first to go outside and hire Jay. But his name kept coming up. And through the grapevine I learned he was the writer behind some big successes at some very big mailers. So I decided to give him a chance — only to discover he was booked solid. Then I found myself contacting him again and again, trying to get him to accept us as a client. When Jay began working on our website and several brochures, we gained an incredible amount of practical sales strategy from him. The bottom line is always results, and Jay gets that for us."

Matthew Day
Director of Business Development, New York Vacation Club

Jay is the "Go-To" Guy for Copy That Sells

"A lot of copywriters can write cute copy or the corporate-speak copy. We see this kind of drivel all the time, and I'm always surprised when these guys and gals stay in business. Jay is truly different. His copy is clever, interesting, and fun, and it really hits the emotional sweet spots. The radio and TV spots that Jay has written and produced with us have all had their own unique persuasive approach. And when his copy makes his clients look good, that makes us look good. We want to work with people we like, and Jay is one of my favorites."

Robin Russ
Vice President, Studio Center

Jay, Let Me Tell You What I Really Think of You

"Jay, initially, I thought your fees were too high, your terms were unreasonable, it was hard to get a slot in your busy schedule, and you were too dogmatic about what you believed worked and why. I really didn't want to hire you. The only thing I thought you had going in your favor was that the numerous advertising agencies and freelancers we had previously tried produced zero results at all. I was determined to take advantage of your money-back guarantee if I had to. I didn't have to. What I discovered is what I thought was all wrong. Your fees weren't too high, because everything you did made us a profit. It was like your services were free. Your terms weren't unreasonable because you know what you're doing, and quite frankly, we don't know how to do what you do. And the reason you are so hard to get ahold of is everyone is trying to get ahold of you because your stuff is proven to work. And I'm not going to say anything about you thinking you're right about everything because I don't want to give you any more ammunition to raise your fees on us. Just keep doing what you're doing. Get us results, and we'll be happy. Thanks for everything."

Ed Lett
CEO and President, TIB Financial Corp.

Jay, You're a Hall of Fame Copywriter

"Jay, I love the letters, and I like how all I had to do was sign my name. The script and the brochure are first-rate, too. I also appreciate all the help you gave me during the shoot. You got what you wanted, even if it was in just one take, and you kept things moving. And you were clever with how you handled the agency suits. I was particularly impressed with how you handled their desire to change the ending of the video. I've had marketing guys I've worked with pitch fits, storm out of the room, or simply try to b.s. me into buying into their rationale when I suggest a change. I like how you seemed to do everything they asked

for, and then cleverly got me to agree with subtle changes that turned it back into what you originally wanted. You should be in the hall of fame just for that."

Pat Summerall
Hall of Fame Sportscaster, Commercial Spokesman

Jay Will Get the Most Potential and Profits from Your Business

"Jay, you really know how to write for business for fast results. I like that you take time to listen and understand our business and how we operate. I think it is vital to look at every aspect of a business and not just the staff's opinions. You helped me set up a system for developing good relationships with customers and an effective plan for achieving more growth. I believe any company can see exactly how you can help them increase their profits and create wealth for themselves if they will hire you to craft a plan for them."

Wallace Parker
Marketing Director, The Florida Times-Union

Jay is Always 5 Stars and Nothing Less

"Jay is instrumental in causing the important marketing shifts that get your business and the people who do your advertising to see things from the customers' perspective. If you're serious about marketing your business successfully and intelligently, Jay will give you the plain truth. Jay made us think. He challenged our assumptions about our business and our market. Jay's guidance is a primary factor in why our communications programs and training programs have been so successful. We still sometimes struggle, but we now have far more ups than downs."

Frank J. Liska
Director, Corporate Communications
Johnson & Johnson

ABOUT THE AUTHOR

Jay Huling, "The Consulting Copywriter"

To people in the know in marketing circles, Jay is a much-sought-after copywriter and trusted marketing consultant. During his 30-plus years of in-the-trenches experience writing for successful companies such as AAA, AARP, Aflac, Cigna, Citibank, CSX, Johnson & Johnson, Horace Mann, Pitney Bowes, Physicians Mutual, Wounded Warrior Project — and more than 300 others — Jay has perfected his direct response style that routinely achieves outstanding results. His monthly newsletter THE HULING LETTER reaches small business owners and entrepreneurs all over the United States, offering tips and advice for turning marketing dollars into business profit. For a FREE copy of his business marketing success kit, *Jay Huling Presents Everything You Want to Know About Getting More Business for Your Business,*" email your request to jay@jayhuling.com.

Jay Huling
The Consulting Copywriter
P.O. Box 14171
Jacksonville, Florida 32238
jay@jayhuling.com
www.jayhuling.com
Call toll-free: 1-800-603-COPY (2679)

ALSO BY JAY HULING

Your Business is in Trouble

Who Will YOU Pay to Create YOUR Marketing and Advertising?

Are the marketing experts you hire really experts?

Or are they just out-of-work frauds masquerading as advertising and branding gurus?

If you're worried that your business has a marketing problem, the truth is you're probably being played.

www.ingramcontent.com/pod-product-compliance
Lightning Source LLC
Chambersburg PA
CBHW021413210526
45463CB00001B/343